Making Friends

ParentsCAN
3299 Claremont Way, Ste.3
Napa, CA 94558

FIRST EXPERIENCES

Making Friends

BY FRED ROGERS

photographs by Jim Judkis

The Putnam & Grosset Group

With special thanks to: Nan Earl Newell;
Margaret B. McFarland, Ph.D., Senior Consultant;
Barry N. Head; the Azocar family; the Gerber family;
and the other parents and children who agreed
to help us with the book.

Printed on recycled paper

A PaperStar Book, published in 1996 by The Putnam & Grosset Group,
200 Madison Avenue, New York, NY 10016. PaperStar Books and
the PaperStar logo are trademarks of The Putnam Berkley Group, Inc.
Originally published in 1987 by G.P. Putnam's Sons.
Published simultaneously in Canada.
Printed in the United States of America.
Library of Congress Cataloging-in-Publication Data
Rogers, Fred. Making friends.
(A Mister Rogers' First experience book)
At head of title: Mister Rogers' neighborhood.
Summary: Explains what it means to be friends and
some of the easy and difficult aspects of friendship.
1. Friendship—Juvenile literature.   [1. Friendship]
I. Judkis, Jim, ill.   II. Mister Rogers' neighborhood
(Television program)   III. Title.   IV. Series: Rogers, Fred.
Mister Rogers' First experience book.
BJ1533.F8R66   1987   177.6 86-12353
ISBN 0-698-11409-4
1   3   5   7   9   10   8   6   4   2

One of life's greatest joys is the comfortable give-and-take of a good friendship. It is a wonderful feeling not only to have a good friend but to know how to be a good friend yourself.

Learning about friendship begins at an early age when children "graduate" from playing side by side to playing *with* each other. There is so much to learn about sharing toys and sharing loved ones as children begin to share themselves with others.

It can be disheartening for a parent to watch a toddler fighting over a toy or jostling for a first place in line. Nonetheless, learning to share and learning to compromise are enormous challenges for the young child whose view of the world is still largely self-centered. Our adult patience and realistic expectations can be as helpful to the child as knowing when we ought to step in and mediate a dispute.

A good friend of mine once remarked that "character is caught, not taught." I think that is also true of empathy and tolerance and the other things that have to do with being a good friend . . . they're all caught, not taught.

We can provide our children with opportunities for play with their peers. We can offer them suggestions for compromise, and we can intervene when necessary. But our greatest gift may be the examples we set in our own friendships. It is from us, I believe, that our children are likely to learn best.

—Fred Rogers

When people like each other and like to do things together, they're friends. Can you think of someone who's your friend?

That friend might be a boy
or a girl your own age . . .

Or someone older . . .
or younger.

You might be friends with someone in your neighborhood . . .

. . . or at school.

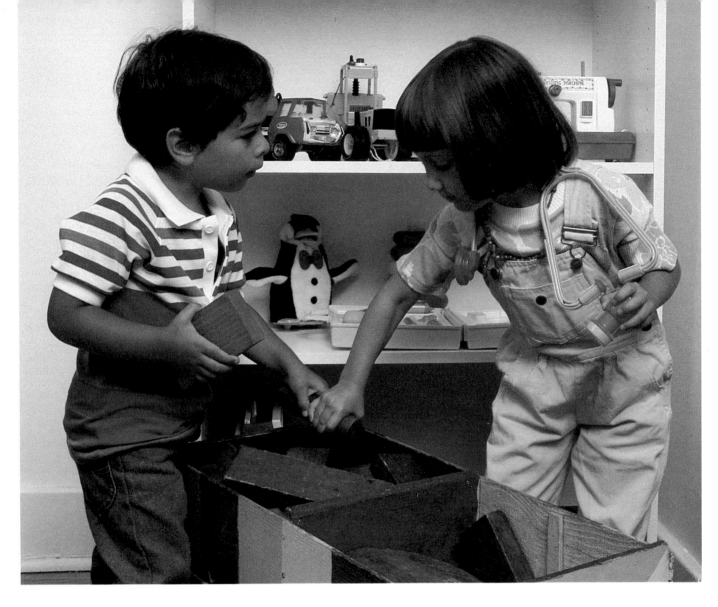

There are times when friends like to do the same things and other times when they don't. It isn't always easy for friends to decide what they want to do when they're together.

When you're playing by yourself, you can do things your own way. You have your own toys, and you can have your own ideas about how to play with them.

When you're playing with a friend, that friend might want to do things another way. After all, no two people are exactly alike, so nobody does things exactly the same way.

When one friend tries hard to do things one way and another friend tries hard to do things *another* way, those friends can get angry with each other.

But when they can finally decide how they want to play, they can get new ideas from each other.

It can be hard to share your toys, and it can be hard to wait your turn—even for friends.

When you *can* share or wait your turn, you can know that you're learning how to be a good friend.

When you and your friend are playing
together, is it sometimes hard to let
someone else play, too?

When your friend decides to play
with someone else for a while, do
you ever feel that you aren't
friends anymore?

Well, to be friends, the same people don't have to play together *all* the time, and it can be a good feeling to know that you can have more than *one* friend.

Good friends can have lots of happy times together—

Times when they go
somewhere special . . .

Times when they discover something new.

Times when they share a secret.

And times when they try to help each other feel better.

Good friends can make each other laugh or smile, and sometimes they might even feel like being silly.

But good friends can also make each other very angry or sad. Even a good friend could make you feel so bad you wish the whole world would go away—or so mad you might feel like hitting or pushing everybody in sight.

When children feel like that, they can tell the people they love about it. Grownups can understand because they were little once, too, and they've had times when they've been sad or mad. It isn't always easy to talk about those feelings, but often it can help.

When you have those sad or mad feelings, the people
you love can help you do things that won't hurt you
or anyone else.